P9-DHK-204

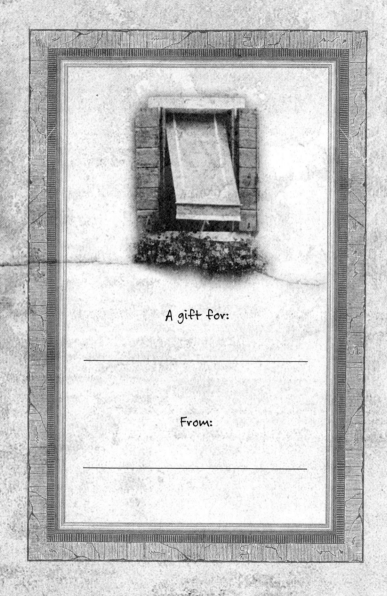

A gift for:

_____

From:

_____

encouragement
for life

words of hope and inspiration

Charles R. Swindoll

Contents

Preface

Encourage me.

Maybe you haven't said those words out loud in recent days, but chances are you have shaped them in the silent hallways of your soul.

Maybe you haven't stopped anyone on the street and said that phrase. But if someone cared enough to look closely they would see the words written in your sad face, drooping shoulders, and pleading eyes. They would hear the words echo in your unguarded comments and unsuppressed sighs.

Is that where you've been lately? Are you running shy on reinforcement and affirmation? Are you beginning to wonder not *when* relief is coming, but *if* it will ever come? Then I believe this little book will help. I am writing it with people like you in mind. People who feel riveted to the valley where the sun seldom shines and others seldom care.

I do not write out of sterile theory but out of reality. My pen has been dipped in a deep well. The ink has been dark and often cold. At such times I have struggled with a lack of self worth . . . a common battle waged in the valley. The long shadows of discouragement have often stretched across my path. Those times have been bittersweet—bitter at first, sweet later on.

I have only one goal in mind: to encourage you. Tired, discouraged friend, take heart! The Lord God can and will lift you up! There is no pit so deep that He is not deeper still. No valley so dark that the light of His truth cannot penetrate.

Encouragement.

If you miss it and need it and want it, read on. And if you find it, by all means share it with others!

CHARLES R. SWINDOLL

We are never closer to
God than when trials
come upon us.

Take God seriously,
but don't take
yourself too
seriously.

Chapter One

ENCOURAGEMENT
FOR SELF-DOUBT
AND INSECURITY

What Incredible Worth!

Possessions of the powerful, wealthy, or famous, no matter how common, can become extremely valuable, even priceless. Napoleon's toothbrush sold for $21,000. Can you imagine paying thousands of dollars for someone's cruddy old toothbrush? Hitler's car sold for over $150,000. Winston Churchill's desk, a pipe owned by C. S. Lewis, sheet music handwritten by Beethoven, a house once owned by Ernest Hemingway. At the Sotheby's auction of Jackie Kennedy Onassis's personal belongings, her fake pearls sold for $211,500 and JFK's wood golf clubs went for $772,500. Not because the items themselves are worthy but because they once belonged to someone significant.

Are you ready for a surprise? We fit that bill too. Think of the value of something owned by God. What incredible worth that bestows on us, what inexplicable dignity! We belong to Him. We are "a people for God's own possession" (1 Pet. 2:9).

The price paid for us was unimaginably high—the blood of Jesus Christ—and now we belong to Him. We have been bought with a price. That's enough to bring a smile to anyone's face. But there is more. . . .

As a result of God's mercy, we have become a people who are uniquely and exclusively cared for by God. The fact that we are the recipients of His mercy makes all the difference in the world as to how we respond to difficult times. He watches over us with enormous interest. Why? Because of His immense mercy, freely demonstrated in spite of our not deserving it. What guilt-relieving, encouraging news!

HOPE AGAIN

AN ENCOURAGING WORD:

Freedom

Be who you are. Give
yourself the O.k. to break
the mold and exercise your
God-given freedom.

God, in grace, has
purchased you from
bondage. Christ has
literally set you free.

Sometimes it's encouraging just
to thumb through the Scriptures
and find all the promises that
tell us what God thinks of us,
especially in a world where
folks are continually telling
us all the things they have
against us and all the
things they see
wrong with us.

He has made us to be a kingdom,
priests to His God and Father.

REVELATION 1:6

You formed my inward parts;
You wove me in my mother's womb.

PSALM 139:13

We love, because He first loved us.

1 JOHN 4:19

God's Power and Strength

nadequacy. Simply reading the word arouses an array of emotions. Very few on this earth are immune to this struggle, even those whom others think are strong and self-sufficient.

> ➤ Inadequate as mothers to care every day for busy, demanding toddlers
> ➤ Inadequate to speak in public
> ➤ Inadequate to confront a difficult employee
> ➤ Inadequate to stop a longstanding habit or addiction
> ➤ Inadequate to learn a new job after being laid off
> ➤ Inadequate to stay in a marriage that continues to be unfulfilling
> ➤ Inadequate to take care of aging parents or all those teenagers
> ➤ Inadequate to go on living when every dream has crashed and burned

It's always something! Take it from me, even those who exude an air of confidence and poise secretly struggle with inadequacy.

Let's face it: To be human is to feel inadequate.

Everywhere we look we discover human inadequacy. Obviously, not all of us struggle against severe physical weakness. But the fact is, we are weak—emotionally, spiritually, intellectually, and mentally. We are incapable of glorifying God in and of ourselves. We are unable to do His work our own way and in our own strength. If we are going to be His arms and His legs, His voice and His presence, it will happen only through His assistance. That's why He allows our feelings of inadequacy. Inadequacy forces us to rely fully on God for power and strength.

Not surprisingly, that's a truth Christ's disciples struggled to embrace, especially after being commissioned to span the world and proclaim God's light amid immense spiritual darkness. Can you imagine their confusion when the full load of Christ's divine commission landed on them? Don't forget, they heard it first as Jesus was leaving the earth!

Jesus was asking the impossible of the tiny band of reluctant evangelists. But that was precisely the point. They needed His power to accomplish His command. They needed to be transformed. May I remind you? So do we!

All the hoping and dreaming in the world won't make it possible for me to sit down at a piano and play a Beethoven sonata like Van Cliburn. Nice idea but an impossible notion. But if the world-renowned pianist were somehow able to confer on me all the skill and brilliance of his ability, undergirded by his decades of study and practice and magnificent talent, perhaps I could pull it off. But make no mistake, that would require a transfer of Van Cliburn's musical genius into my very being. I would need his spirit within me, literally.

That's what we face in the Christian life. Christ has given us His power through the infilling presence of the Holy Spirit. The Holy Spirit indwells us when we turn to God through faith in His Son. No need to pray, dance, hope, shout, or plead for divine power. If you are a follower of Christ, you have Christ's power in you. The Holy Spirit literally resides within your being. The more you yield your life to Him, the more His power flows through you. He is there, ready and able to empower us. Is that great news or what?

If you have retreated to the back alley of life and are wallowing in all your inadequacies, then you're exactly where God needs you to be to demonstrate His power. It's time to kneel humbly before Him and let go. Release your grip. Pour out your heart.

You have a Savior who is waiting to demonstrate His great power in you. Don't waste another minute trying to get through the tough stuff of inadequacy on your own. Don't run away from this test. Run to Him and receive His power.

GETTING THROUGH THE TOUGH STUFF

My Grace is sufficient for you, for
power is perfected in weakness.

2 CORINTHIANS 12:9

AN ENCOURAGING WORD:

Strength

We have the greatest
confidence in God's Spirit
to provide the strength
we'll need to face
whatever lies ahead.

God Sees and Cares

God knows, right down to the final nub, exactly where you are in life. He sees. He cares. He is aware. And best of all, He is touched by it.

The enemy of our souls wants you to think differently. *God doesn't care. He's left you in this mess for so many months. How unfair! Those around you, those at work, your neighbors, live like the devil, and they're making it fine. And here you don't even have a job. You don't even have enough to cover the credit card bills. What kind of God is that?*

Or maybe some young mother-to-be, stretched to the limit already with other young children and crushing responsibilities, cries out in her heart, "My situation is more than I can bear!" And God replies, "My daughter, I know what I am doing. I know the pain of your heart right now. I know you feel overwhelmed, overloaded, pressed down. But believe Me, I am touched with your situation. And I have a plan! I am working out the details of your deliverance even now. Trust Me!

Moses: A Man of Selfless Dedication

God Wants You to Be YOU

There is only one YOU.

Think about that. Your face and features, your voice, your style, your background, your characteristics and peculiarities, your abilities, your smile, your walk, your handshake, your manner of expression, your viewpoint . . . everything about you is found in only one individual *since man first began*—YOU.

How does that make you feel? Frankly, I'm elated!

Dig as deeply as you please in the ancient, dusty archives of *Homo sapiens* and you'll not find another YOU in the whole lot. And that, by the way, did not "just happen"; it was planned that way. Why? Because God wanted you to be YOU, that's why. He designed you to be a unique, distinct, significant person unlike any other individual on the face of the earth, throughout the vast expanse of time. In your case, as in the case of every other human being, the mold was broken, never to be used again, once you entered the flow of mankind.

Consider David's perspective on this subject:

You formed my inward parts;
You wove me in my mother's womb.
I will give thanks to You, for I am
Fearfully and wonderfully made.
Wonderful are Your works,
And my soul knows it very well.
My frame was not hidden from You,
When I was made in secret,
And skillfully wrought in the
Depths of the earth;
Your eyes have seen my unformed substances;
And in Your book were all written
The days that were ordained for me,
When as yet there was not one of them.

PSALM 139: 13–16

If I read this astounding statement correctly, you were prescribed and then presented to this world exactly as God arranged it. Reflect on that truth, discouraged friend. Read David's words one more time, and don't miss the comment that God is personally involved in the very days and details of your life. Great thought!

In our overly-populated, identity-crises era, it is easy to forget this. Individuality is played down. We are asked to conform to the "system." Group opinion is considered superior to personal conviction and everything from the college fraternity to the businessman's service club tends to encourage our blending into the mold of the masses.

It's okay to "do your own thing" just so long as it is similar to others when they do "their own thing." Any other thing is the wrong thing. Hogwash!

My mind lands upon a fig-picker from Tekoa . . . a rough, raw-boned shepherd who was about as subtle as a Mack truck on the Santa Ana Freeway. He was tactless, unsophisticated, loud, uneducated, and uncooperative. His name was Amos. That was no problem. He was a preacher. That *was* a problem. He didn't fit the image . . . but he refused to let that bother him.

He was called (of all things) to bring the morning messages in the king's sanctuary. And bring them he did. His words penetrated those vaulted ceilings and icy pews like flaming arrows. In his own way, believing firmly in his message, he pounced upon sin like a hen on a June bug . . . the "image keepers" of Israel told him to be silent, to peddle his doctrine of doom in the backwoods of Judah. His rugged style didn't fit in with the plush, "royal residence" at Bethel (Amos 7:12–13).

Aware of their attempt to straight-jacket his method and restructure his message, Amos replied:

> "I am not a prophet, nor am I the son of a prophet; for
> I am a herdsman and a grower of sycamore figs.
> But the LORD took me from following the
> flock and the LORD said to me, 'Go
> prophesy to My people Israel.'"

AMOS 7:14–15

You don't "fit the mold"? Is that what sent you down into the valley of discouragement? You don't sound like every other Christian or look like the "standard" saint . . . or act like the majority?

Hallelujah! Don't sweat it, my friend. And don't you dare change just because you're outnumbered. Then you wouldn't be YOU.

What the world needs is a lot more faithful fig-pickers who have the courage to simply be themselves, regardless.

You are YOU. There is only YOU. And YOU are important.

Want to start feeling better? Really desire to dispel discouragement? I can say it all in three words:

Start being YOU!

ENCOURAGE ME

Fun

There is an old Greek motto
that says: You will break the
bow if you keep it always bent.

Which, being loosely translated,
means, "There's more to life
than hard work." Loosening the
strings on our bow means when
we have some leisure, we live it
up. We deliberately erase from
our minds that we are a cop
or a nurse or a lawyer or a
preacher. We do stuff
that helps us stay sane.
And fun to be with.

The hope of the
righteous is gladness.

Affirmation and Appreciation

All of us need encouragement—somebody to believe in us. To reassure and reinforce us. To help us pick up the pieces and go on. To provide us with increased determination in spite of the odds. . . .

When we encourage others we spur them on, we stimulate and affirm them. It is helpful to remember the distinction between appreciation and affirmation. We appreciate what a person *does*, but we affirm who a person *is*. Appreciation comes and goes because it is usually related to something someone accomplishes. Affirmation goes deeper. It is directed to the person himself or herself. While encouragement would encompass both, the rarer of the two is affirmation. To be appreciated, we get the distinct impression that we must earn it by some accomplishment. But affirmation requires no such prerequisite. This means that even when we don't earn the right to be appreciated (because we failed to succeed or because we lacked the accomplishment of some goal), we can still be affirmed—indeed, we need it then more than ever.

I do not care how influential or secure or mature a person may appear to be, genuine encouragement never fails to help. Most of us need massive doses of it.

STRENGTHENING YOUR GRIP

I'm convinced that one
of the best things God
does for us is to keep us
from knowing what will
happen beyond today.

I know the plans I have for you . . .
plans to prosper you and not to
harm you, plans to give you
hope and a future.

JEREMIAH 29:11   NIV

AN ENCOURAGING WORD:

Courage

It's impossible to live victoriously
for Christ without courage.

Have you ever been around
a person of faith? Ever rubbed
shoulders with men and women
of God who didn't have the word
"impossible" in their vocabulary?
It's the most incredible
association you can imagine.
It's remarkable how it builds
courage into your faith!

We are not in the
hands of blind fate!
We are in the
hands of God.

Chapter Two

ENCOURAGEMENT
FOR DESPAIR AND DOUBT

Focus First on God

G od is the Potter; we are the clay.
He's the Shepherd; we are the sheep.
He's the Master; we are the servant.

No matter how educated we are, no matter how much power and influence we may think we have, no matter how long we have walked with Him, no matter how significant we may imagine ourselves to be in His plans (if any of us could even claim significance), none of that qualifies us to grasp the first particle of why He does what He does when He does it and how He chooses to do it. . . .

There is a mystery, an aura about the living God that is designed to force us to trust Him, even when we cannot figure Him out (which is most of the time). . . .

The mystery is purposeful, because His overall plan is profound. . . . His plan is not designed to make us comfortable; it's designed to make us more like Christ, to conform us to His will. . . .

In this life, we have focus choices. We can focus on ourselves, we can focus on our circumstances, we can focus on other people, or we can focus on God. When you think biblically you focus first on God. Regardless of what you want, regardless of the circumstances you're under, regardless of what others say or think, regardless of how you feel, God and God alone is working out His great plan. And in the final tally, it will be fabulous!

THE MYSTERY OF GOD'S WILL

Do not fear, for I am with you.

ISAIAH 41:10

God knows where we are. Sometimes we
forget this. Sometimes we even feel that God
has forgotten us. He hasn't. God knows exactly
where we are. So when you are afflicted with
those forsaken feelings, when you're on the
verge of throwing a pity party, thanks to
those despairing thoughts, go back
to the Word of God. God says,
"I know where you are."

Those also who suffer
according to the will of
God shall entrust their souls
to a faithful Creator in
doing what is right.

1 PETER 4:19

AN ENCOURAGING WORD:

Entrust

Entrust. What a wonderful
word! It is a banking term
in the original text,
meaning "to deposit."

When it comes to trials, we
deposit ourselves into God's
safekeeping and that deposit
yields eternal dividends.

Baffled by Life's Mysteries?

S ir Winston Churchill was seldom at a loss for words. Whether he was making a brief comment to the press or delivering a lengthy address before Parliament, the late British statesman distinguished himself as a master of the English language. He seemed never at a loss for words—except when it came to an explanation of the actions of Russia.

Neither the French nor the Americans baffled him. Not even Nazi Germany left him bewildered. But Russia's unpredictable and illogical actions frequently threw him for a loop. On one occasion as he found himself once again confounded by the Soviets' surprising decision, he exclaimed in utter frustration, "It is a riddle, wrapped up in a mystery, inside an enigma." That's about as complicated as something can get!

Reading over Churchill's descriptive turn of a phrase, you may feel as I do that it's an apt description of many things in life. There are numerous riddles in life that remain riddles wrapped in mystery and shrouded inside an enigma. The sea, for example, is an unexplainable phenomenon. Who can fathom its tide affected strangely by the moon, not to mention its large content of salt, or its incredible swells and currents that form those amazing yet mysterious paths from continent to continent? . . .

Not all mysteries are as profound as that. Some are somewhere between baffling and humorous. There's the mystery of a washing machine for example. Forgive me if this sounds a bit ridiculous, but I would imagine that my home is not that different from yours. We can put in twelve pairs of socks that perfectly match and in some phenomenal, mysterious manner thirty minutes later we remove eight socks, none of which seem to match anything! . . .

We seem to have little trouble going on through life with dozens of riddles still unanswered, hundreds of mysteries still unsolved. But when God leaves us with a mystery that isn't solved in a week or two, most of us go through desperate struggles believing that He is good or fair. I mean, after all, if we're going to trust a good God, He should do only good things, right? No fair doing mysterious stuff!

The Bible that I read simply doesn't present that as the way life is. . . . Actually the Bible is full of mysteries. I find the mystery of the kingdom in the first chapter of the gospel of Mark. There is the mystery of Israel in Romans 11 and the mystery of resurrection in 1 Corinthians 15. The little letter to the Ephesians mentions no less than four mysteries. Second Thessalonians presents the mystery of lawlessness, and Paul mentions the mystery of godliness in 1 Timothy 3. God's Word, like God's will, is full of mysteries.

Why should we be surprised, then, when God steps in and does mysterious things? Why should that make us wonder if He is good—or wonder if we want to keep believing? Since when must everything be easily or logically explained? . . .

All of us have had mysteries of some kind that have invaded our lives. No doubt you have had things happen that have shaken and stunned you. And perhaps you've decided to wait until God unfolds the meaning of the drama. And the longer you wait, the less you seem to grasp why. And the further you seek to understand why, the more oblique the mystery becomes.

So how do we handle the mysteries? What do we do with those unsolved questions? What do we do with unjust triumphs and with unfair consequences?

I have come up with three suggestions that might answer those questions:

1. *We must each admit: "I am only human"—and admit it daily.* We must not become so impressed with our spiritual redemption that we forget that we are human, finite, and fallible.
2. *We must each admit: "I don't understand why—and I may never on this earth learn why."* We must then try our best, by the power of God, not to let that affect our faith. In fact, we should ask God to use that lack of knowledge to deepen our faith.

3. *We must each admit: "I cannot bring about a change."* We may have tried. We may have done everything we know to do—but we can't change this situation. It is time to admit, "I have no power to change it . . . Lord, God, You know what is best for Your child. I wait. This is what You have given me under the sun. I will walk in it." And that explains how the Christian can have joy in the midst of wild and crazy, mysterious and strained circumstances.

When we respond to mysteries in this manner, we no longer struggle with unjust triumph and unfair consequences. And as a result, *we'll* become a mystery. Our untimely pleasure will create all kinds of interest in the phenomena of how we think. We will have doors opened to us.

That, dear friend, is the way to live. Through all the misery and the mysteries—to trust in Jesus and depend upon His Word.

LIVING ON THE RAGGED EDGE

God never forgets anything He
promises. That's right . . . never.

God's Ways Are Higher

D r. Bruce Waltke was my Hebrew professor during three of my years at Dallas Seminary. He has since become something of a mentor and friend. He is a brilliant man with a tender heart for God. When I was going through a very difficult time in my senior year in seminary and wanted some answers to the *whys*, Bruce said something like this: "Chuck, I've come to the place where I believe only on very rare occasions does God tell us why, so I've decided to stop asking." I found that to be very helpful counsel. From that point on, I began to acknowledge that I am not the "answer man" for events in life that don't make logical, human sense. I'm now convinced that even if God did explain His reasons, I would seldom understand. His ways are higher and far more profound than our finite minds can comprehend. So I now accept God's directions, and I live with them as best I can. And frankly, I leave it at that.

HOPE AGAIN

AN ENCOURAGING WORD:

Stability

There's a sense of stability
in trusting the Lord. That's
how we wait silently and with
a sense of confidence. When
we wait for God to direct our
steps, He does! When we trust
Him to meet our needs, He will!

Fix Your Eyes on the Lord

Until your eyes are fixed on the Lord, you will not be able to endure those days that go from bad to worse.

Fix your eyes on the Lord! Do it first. Do it daily. Do it ten thousand times ten thousand times. Do it constantly. When your schedule presses, when your prospects thin, when your hope burns low, when people disappoint you, when events turn against you, when dreams die, when the walls close in, when the prognosis seems grim, when your heart breaks, *look at the Lord, and keep on looking at Him.*

Who is He? He is Yahweh, the eternal I AM, the sovereign Lord of the universe. He cannot do what is unjust; it is against His nature. He has never lost control. He is always faithful. Changeless. All powerful. All knowing. Good. Compassionate. Gracious. Wise. Loving. Sovereign. Reliable.

As Peter put it, "Lord to whom shall we go? You have words of eternal life" (John 6:68). He's right. There really is nowhere else to turn and no one else to turn to.

MOSES: A MAN OF SELFLESS DEDICATION

Happily Ever After?

An old French fairy tale tells the story of two daughters—one bad and the other good. The bad daughter was the favorite of her mother, but the good daughter was unjustly neglected, despised, and mistreated.

One day, while drawing water from the village well, the good daughter met a poor woman who asked for a drink. The girl responded with kind words and gave the woman a cup of water. The woman, actually a fairy in disguise, was so pleased with the little girl's kindness and good manners that she gave her a gift.

"Each time you speak," said the woman, "a flower or jewel will come out of your mouth."

When the little girl got home, her mother began to scold her for taking so long to bring the water. The girl started to apologize, and two roses, two pearls, and two diamonds came out of her mouth.

Her mother was astonished. But after hearing her daughter's story and seeing the number of beautiful jewels that came out in the telling, the mother called her other daughter and sent her forth to get the same gift. The bad daughter, however, was reluctant to be seen performing the lowly task of drawing water, so she grumbled sourly all the way to the well.

When the bad daughter got to the well, a beautiful queenly woman—that same fairy in another disguise—came by and asked for a drink. Disagreeable and proud, the girl responded rudely. As a result, she received her reward too. Each time she opened her mouth, she emitted snakes and toads.

How's that for poetic justice!

There's something in each one of us that longs for circumstances to be fair, isn't there? Maybe that's why fairy tales are so appealing. Good people receive their rewards and "live happily ever after" while bad people are soundly punished. Life works out, justice is done, and fairness reigns supreme.

Unfortunately, real life doesn't usually turn out that way.

HOPE AGAIN

The happiest people
I know are the ones
who have learned how
to hold everything loosely
and have given the worrisome,
stress-filled, fearful details of
their lives into God's keeping.

Joy

Remember when Paul and
Silas were seized by a hostile
mob, dragged into a public
marketplace, beaten mercilessly,
then dumped into a dungeon
with their feet fastened in
stocks? As you may recall, it was
around midnight at the end of
that same day, while their sores
were oozing and their bruises
throbbing, that he and Silas
were praying and singing
a few duets of praise.

What contagious joy!

God Gives the Joy

I know that there is nothing better
for them than to rejoice and to do good
in one's lifetime. . . . It is the gift of God.

ECCLESIASTES 3:12–13

God gives us the ability to rejoice and enjoy life.
Have you ever seen a person who didn't have the
Lord really and truly enjoying life on a regular basis? How
about the one who has no place in his or her life for God?
Have you ever known one individual like that who was
continually rejoicing? I haven't either.

The only one who enjoys and exudes the gift of rejoicing is
the believer. Why? Because God alone can give the perspective
and refreshing hope needed to sustain a life of joy, regardless,
and I do mean regardless.

I heard about a man who gave his business to God. He
had hassled over it for years. He had wrestled with the many
decisions and fought the financial challenges for two decades.
One day he decided, "I've had it; that's enough!" He had heard

from his pastor on Sunday morning about the value of turning his entire business over to God. As he drove away from church he decided he had worried enough. By the time he got home, he had totally and unequivocally committed his business to God.

That very night his place of business caught on fire. He got an emergency call. He rather calmly drove down to the commercial building and stood on the street, watching the place go up in flames. He was sort of smiling to himself. One of his colleagues raced to his side and questioned his relaxed attitude about what was happening. "Man! Don't you know what háppened to you . . . It's . . . it's burning up!"

He replied, "I know it. I know it. No problem, Fred. This morning I gave this company to God, and if He wants to burn it up, that's His business."

Not even a fire, not even a disaster like that is sufficient to take the gift of rejoicing from you when God gives it to you!

LIVING ON THE RAGGED EDGE

In Me you may have peace. In the world you have tribulation, but take courage; I have overcome the world.

JOHN 16:33

Invisible Bridges

When will we ever learn that there are no hopeless situations, only people who have grown hopeless about them? What appears as an unsolvable problem to us is actually a rather exhilarating challenge. People who inspire others are those who see invisible bridges at the end of dead-end streets.

There was a Cabinet meeting in London during the darkest days of the Second World War. France had just capitulated. Prime Minister Churchill outlined the situation in its starkest colors. Quite literally, the tiny British Isles stood alone. Grim faces stared back at him in stoic silence. Despair and thoughts of surrender were written in their looks. The visionary statesman momentarily remained silent, lit a cigar, showed a hint of a smile, and with a twinkle in his eye, responded to that dispirited company of officials, "Gentlemen, I find it rather inspiring." He was the one who, on another occasion, said, "Nothing in life is so exhilarating as to be shot at without result." What a great line! No wonder people followed the man. Fear of failure never entered his mind!

Dropping Your Guard

Everything Is Under Control

At the heart of life's major struggles is a theological issue. Putting it in the form of a question: "Is God in charge or is He not?"

If we could, by some wonderful force from heaven, be allowed to slip from this earth in our present state and into the glory of heaven, we would not find one shred of evidence that reveals panic. You would never once hear "oops" from the lips of God, or "I wonder what we're going to do about that down there?" Nor would we ever observe anxiety across the face of the living God. We would be stunned with amazement at how calm things are around His awesome throne.

From this side of glory we see the tapestry of life from underneath. It is full of knots and twisted threads and frayed ends that lack meaning and beauty. But from God's perspective, looking at the top of the fabric, it is all under control.

LIVING ON THE RAGGED EDGE

Thank the Lord, it is His *love* that arranges our tomorrows and whatever they bring.

Written on the Palms of His Hands

"The Lord has forsaken me . . . He has walked away . . . He has totally forgotten me." Ever said that? Of course you have! How about on Monday morning? You've just come off a glorious weekend retreat. Time in the Word. Great worship. . . . lots of laughter. Meaningful prayer. . . . Then comes eight o'clock Monday morning back home, and your whole *world* caves in. "The Lord's forgotten me. He's completely left the scene."

But God says, "You are written on the palms of My hands. You are continually before me." . . .

Stop and glance at the palms of your hand. Now, imagine they are God's hands and that you are right there. . . . Our ways remain continually before Him. Not one fleeting moment of life goes by without His knowing exactly where we are, what we're doing, and how we're feeling.

ELIJAH: A MAN OF HEROISM & HUMILITY

"I will not forget you! See, I have engraved you on the palms of my hands."

ISAIAH 49:16 NIV

To increase your passion
for life, I have some
pretty simple advice:
Be ready for anything.

Chapter Three

ENCOURAGEMENT
FOR INDECISION
AND UNCERTAINTY

Our Will or God's Will?

As children of God, our greatest desire should be to do God's will. And in our most thoughtful, mature moments, we want to do His will. . . .

But doing the will of God is rarely easy and uncomplicated. Instead, it is often difficult and convoluted. Or, to use my preferred term, it is *mysterious*. Because we don't know where He is taking us, we must bend our wills to His—and most of us are not all that excited about bending. We'd much prefer resisting. That's why the Christian life is often such a struggle. I don't mean that it's a constant marathon of misery. It's just a struggle between our will and His will.

At the fork of every road, we need faith and action to follow God's leading. That is the crisis of belief. It is a turning point, where we must make a decision.

One person who struggled with a crisis of belief was Sarah, Abraham's wife. "You will have a baby," God promised. Many years passed but she didn't conceive. Finally, she decided to take control of her own destiny. She told Abraham, "Go in to my handmaiden, Hagar, and have the child by her." Dumb decision. Instead of waiting for God's plan and timing, she rushed ahead and pushed Hagar into Abraham's tent. And to complicate things, Abraham foolishly cooperated. The result was Ishmael, and we all know where that led. The conflict that resulted between the descendants of Ishmael and the descendants of Isaac has only intensified through the centuries.

God wants us to walk by faith, not by sight. But we're only comfortable when we can see what's ahead, and what's behind, and what's all around us. We want proof. We want guarantees. We much prefer sight to faith.

But God says, "If you're going to please Me, you're going to have to take My Word on this. You're going to have to believe that I am who I say I am, and that I will do what I say I will do." Plain and simple.

Being on the ocean liner of God's will boils down to going where He wants us to go and being what He wants us to be. This means releasing our own plans and pride and will as we flesh out His plan and purpose. In the process, we experience a deep inner peace, a satisfying sense of fulfillment, because we are within the circumference of His plan.

THE MYSTERY OF GOD'S WILL

God never forgets anything He
promises. That's right . . . never.

God's agenda continues
to unfold right on schedule,
even when there is not a shred
of evidence that He remembers.
Even when the most extreme
events transpire and "life just
doesn't seem fair," God is
there, carrying out His
providential plan exactly
as He pre-arranged it.
He keeps His word.

AN ENCOURAGING WORD:

Wisdom

When we find ourselves at
a loss to know what to do or
how to respond, we ask for help.
And God delivers more than
intelligence, ideas, and good
old common sense. He dips into
His well of wisdom and allows
us to drink from His bucket,
whose refreshment provides
abilities and insights that
are of another world.

Wisdom When We Need It

D o you know what I've discovered about the Lord? He doesn't give wisdom on credit. He doesn't advance you a bundle of insight, or slip you several Spirit-filled phrases to tuck away and use in an emergency. Do you know when He gives us words and wisdom and insight? *Right when we need them.* At the very instant they are required.

If you're a parent, you may have experienced this phenomenon. You find yourself in a situation you never anticipated, and couldn't prepare for. Suddenly, you're at one of the critical junctures of life where you're the mom or dad, and your child is looking into your eyes, depending on you for a right answer. Not always, but often, you are given the words you need. Later you realize that they were words beyond your own wisdom. At that quiet moment, you breathe a little prayer of thanks. "Praise You, Lord. That's exactly what needed to be said." You couldn't have planned for it, you couldn't have prepared for it; but when the moment came, the Lord gave you the wisdom and the words you required.

MOSES: A MAN OF SELFLESS DEDICATION

He is the God of your soaring
moments as well as your
perplexing predicaments.

God Knows Your Ways

"*God has the whole world in His hands.*" Remember the old gospel song? He's got the wind, the rain, the tiny little baby, yes, even you and me in His hands. How easy it is to forget that! And it isn't limited to our geography or our culture, you know. He's got the Middle East in His hands (that's a relief, isn't it?), not to mention North Korea and Iran, Cuba and India, Indonesia and Russia—all right there in the palms of His sovereign hands. And while we're at it, He's got our future, our children, our circumstances, our friends, and our foes in His hands . . . within His grasp . . . under His control. Even when imaginary fears slip in like the morning frost to blight our faith, He's there—in charge.

But there are times when we find it really hard to believe that our circumstance is truly in His hands. Not only are the wind and the rain and the tiny little baby in His hands, but so are life's minor interruptions as well as major calamities. In fact, would you believe they never leave His attention?

There will be times we will need the reminder of the wise prophet named Isaiah.

"Behold, I have inscribed you on the palms of My
hands; your walls are continually before Me".

ISAIAH 49:16

In other words, God sees us exactly as we are . . . warts
and all, needs and all. He sees everything. And how close does
He view it? It's in the palms of His hands.

God knows your ways . . . and He knows them *continually*.
That includes your responses, your experiences, your reactions,
what you call your calamities, your dead ends, your so-called
impossible situations.

Not only does He have you and me, the wind and the
rain, and the tiny little baby in His hands, He has yesterday's
failures. He has today's challenges, He has tomorrow's surprises
right there in His hands. And not one of them causes God to
gasp. Not one causes Him to react with surprise, "Ah! I never
knew that." Not one. He is unshockable, He is immutable.
He's got the whole world in His hands. What's more, He has
inscribed you and me on His palms. Things aren't out of control.

LIVING ON THE RAGGED EDGE

AN ENCOURAGING WORD:

Guidance

It is hard to have
dreams dashed, to have
hopes unfulfilled, to face a
future that is unknown and
unfamiliar and sometimes,
if the truth were known,
unwanted. But God has a
way of guiding us unerringly
into the path of righteousness
for His name's sake.

Two Are Better than One

There's an old Swedish motto that hangs in many a kitchen in Scandanavia. It says: "Shared joy is a double joy. Shared sorrow is half a sorrow." Without others, life slows to a grind rather rapidly. As the little kitchen motto states, the secret of survival is not simply enjoying life's joys and enduring its sorrows, it is in sharing both with others.

We gain perspective by having somebody at our side. We gain objectivity. We gain courage in threatening situations. Having others near tempers our dogmatism and softens our intolerance. We gain another opinion. We gain what today, in our technical world, is called "input."

In other words, it is better not to work or live one's life all alone. It's better not to minister all alone. It's better to have someone alongside us in the battle.

There are occasions when we need the embrace of a friend who pulls our head close and whispers in our ear words of understanding, encouraging us not to quit, reminding us that life will go on . . . we will make it. Such embraces put steel into our bones. They help us make it through the night.

If you hope to make it through days of disillusionment and times of trouble, the secret is friendship. Or, to put it in the terms of an equation, "One plus one equals survival." There's no bridge quite like a friend, especially when you're forced to live on the ragged edge of troubled waters.

LIVING ON THE RAGGED EDGE

When the Lord is in it,
anything is possible

Dreams Dressed in Denim

J ust now finishing school? Looking for a job? Is this the reason you're discouraged? Remember this—dreams are great and visions are fun. But in the final analysis, when the bills come due, they'll be paid by manual labor. *Labor* . . . hard work forged in the furnace of practicality. The amazing thing about the practical person—he may not have the most fun or think the deepest thoughts, but he seldom goes hungry!

The Bible is full of men and women who dreamed dreams and saw visions. But they didn't stop there. They had faith, they were people who saw the impossible, and yet their feet were planted on planet earth. You might say they were pragmatic dreamers.

Take Nehemiah. What a man! He had the task of rebuilding the stone wall around Jerusalem. He spent days thinking, praying, observing, dreaming, and planning. But was he ever practical! He organized a large group of unknowns into work parties . . . he faced criticism realistically . . . he stayed at the task without putting out needless fires . . . he met deadlines . . . and he maintained the budget.

Or take Abigail. What a woman! She was married to a first-class jerk, Nabal by name. Because of his lack of wisdom, his greed, prejudice, and selfishness, he roused the ire of his employees. They laid plans to kill him. Being a woman of faith, Abigail thought through the plot, prayed, and planned. Then she did a remarkable thing. She catered a meal to those hungry, angry men. Smart gal! Because of her practicality, Nabal's life was saved and an angry band of men was calmed and turned back.

When it comes to landing a job, most employers are notoriously pragmatic and unsophisticated. They are looking for people who have more than academic, gray winkles between their ears. What they want is someone who can put to use the knowledge that's been gained, whether the field is geology or accounting, engineering or plumbing, physics or medicine, journalism or welding.

That doesn't just happen. People who are in great demand today are those who can see it in their imaginations—then pull it off. Those who can think—then follow through. Those who dress their daring dreams in practical denim work clothes. The pragmatic dreamers. That takes a measure of gift, a pinch of skill, and a ton of discipline!

ENCOURAGE ME

We are only finite human beings. We can only see the present and the past. The future is a little frightening to us. So we need to hold onto God's hand and trust Him to calm our fears.

Faith

- Faith is believing God is who He says He is and that He will do what He says He will do.

- Faith is obeying the Lord when I'm unsure of the outcome.

- Faith is trusting Him when everything in me screams for empirical proof: "Show it to me. Give me the evidence."

- Faith is counting on Him when we do not know what tomorrow holds.

Practical dreamers who proved their detractors wrong:

"Far too noisy, my dear Mozart. Far too many notes."
The Emperor Ferdinand after the first performance of *The Marriage of Figaro*

"If Beethoven's Seventh Symphony is not by some means abridged, it will soon fall into disuse."
Philip Hale, Boston music critic, 1837

"Rembrandt is not to be compared in the painting of character with our extraordinary gifted English artist Mr. Rippingille."
John Hunt (1775–1848)

"Flight by machines heavier than air is unpractical and insignificant . . . utterly impossible."
Simon Newcomb (1835–1909)

"We don't like their sound. Groups of guitars are on their way out."
Decca Recording Company when turning down the Beatles in 1962

"You will never amount to very much."
A Munich schoolmaster to Albert Einstein, age 10

(Adapted from *The Incomplete Book of Failures* by Stephen Pile)

I trust in you, O LORD, . . .
My times are in Your hand.

PSALM 31:14-15

When we are pressed
near the heart of God,
He is faithful and
He will hold us.

Chapter Four

ENCOURAGEMENT
FOR ANXIETY AND WORRY

The Antidote to Worry

While we all have different lists, our deep, relentless worries carry a similar effect. They make us uneasy. They steal smiles from our faces. They cast dark shadows on our futures by spotlighting our shameful pasts. Stubborn anxieties work like petty thieves in the dark corners of our thoughts as they pickpocket our peace and kidnap our joy.

Left to do its insidious work, anxiety will eventually drain us of all resources and leave us emotionally bankrupt and spiritually immobilized, which is why anxiety must be confronted head-on. The first step in that process is to analyze and understand its power.

I have my own definition for anxiety. *Anxiety is the painful uneasiness of the mind that feeds on impending fears.* In its mildest form we simply churn. In its most severe form we panic. This is a good place to pause and dig deeper. Why is anxiety so wrong and spiritually debilitating?

Anxiety highlights the human viewpoint and strangles the divine, so we become fearful. When we worry, we have such a high level of awareness of the human events surrounding us that God's perspective gets choked out. Worry strangles the divine perspective from our daily living, which puts us on edge.

Anxiety chokes our ability to distinguish the incidental from the essential, so we get distracted. In the midst of the worrisome details, we add endless fears, doubts, tasks, expectations, and pressures. Eventually we lose focus on what matters.

Anxiety siphons our joy and makes us judgmental rather than accepting of others, so we become negative. Worry works like bad cholesterol, hardening the arteries of our spiritual hearts and clogging the flow of love and grace toward people. Eventually, as the thorns and thistles intensify, we grow to become negative, bitter, and narrow and basically of little good to anyone.

The antidote to worry?

> Give your entire attention to what God is doing right now, and don't get worked up about what may or may not happen tomorrow. God will help you deal with whatever hard things come up when the time comes.

MATTHEW 6:34 MSG

GETTING THROUGH THE TOUGH STUFF

How wonderful that God personally
cares about those things that
worry us and prey upon our
thoughts. He Cares about
them more than we
care about them.

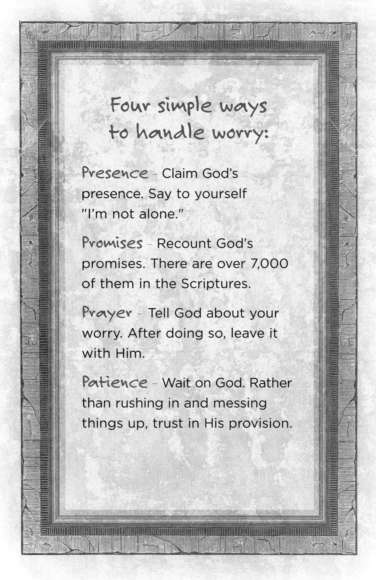

Four simple ways to handle worry:

Presence – Claim God's presence. Say to yourself "I'm not alone."

Promises – Recount God's promises. There are over 7,000 of them in the Scriptures.

Prayer – Tell God about your worry. After doing so, leave it with Him.

Patience – Wait on God. Rather than rushing in and messing things up, trust in His provision.

Ask More

Does God know about the number of hairs in your scalp? Does He care if a sparrow falls? Yes, His Word assures us He does. Then be assured of this: He's a specialist in the things that worry you down inside. The things you dread tomorrow or this coming week. The things that make you wonder, "How can I get this together?" God's reassurance to you is, "Look, that's what I specialize in. I can take that situation you've built into a mountain, and I can bore a tunnel through it in a matter of seconds. Bring all of it to me. Ask Me to take charge. You don't have because you don't ask."

I wonder how many wonderful gifts are left wrapped in heaven because they were never unwrapped on earth? They just remain there, unasked for. James wrote plainly, "You do not have because you do not ask" (James 4:2). In other words, if we would ask more, we would have more. Ask.

PERFECT TRUST

AN ENCOURAGING WORD:

Trustworthy

Let God have His
way with your life.

The amazing thing is that even
in the midst of disappointment,
surprise, and mystery you will
discover how very reliable and
trustworthy God is—and how
secure you are in His hands.

God Understands

J esus says, "O men of little faith. Do not be anxious then, saying, 'What shall we eat?' or 'With what shall we clothe ourselves?'" (Matthew 6:31) The promise of God is that He will not allow His children to beg bread. He will care for our needs and that's the promise you can claim. Since He took care of our greatest need at Calvary by giving us Christ, then you can be sure He will take care of everything else He considers important for us.

This means encouragement if you are in school and beginning to feel overwhelmed with your studies. It's encouragement if you are busily engaged in raising a small family . . . or a large one. It's encouragement if your family is almost gone or perhaps gone already and now you're alone, perhaps without a mate and inclined to worry, "What will I do now?" He understands! He will take care of you!

PERFECT TRUST

God is in sovereign
control of all of life.

Cast all your anxiety on him
because he cares for you.

1 PETER 5:7, NIV

Go Ahead, Call for Help!

A PRAYER TO BE SAID
WHEN THE WORLD HAS GOTTEN YOU DOWN,
AND YOU FEEL ROTTEN,
AND YOU'RE TOO DOGGONE TIRED TO PRAY,
AND YOU'RE IN A BIG HURRY,
AND BESIDES YOU'RE MAD AT EVERYBODY . . .
Help!

Such good counsel. But so tough to carry out. Why is that? Why in the world is it such a struggle for us to cry out for assistance?

- ➤ Ants do it all the time and look at all *they* achieve.
- ➤ In my whole life I have never seen a football game won without substitutions.
- ➤ Even the finest of surgeons will arrange for help in extensive or delicate operations.
- ➤ Highway patrolmen travel in pairs.
- ➤ Through my whole career in the Marin Corps I was drilled to dig a foxhole for *two* in the event of battle.

Asking for help is smart. It's also the answer to fatigue and the "I'm indispensable" image. But something keeps us from this wise course of action, and that something is *pride*. Plain, stubborn unwillingness to admit need. The greatest battle many believers fight today is not with inefficiency, but with *super*-efficiency. It's been bred into us by high-achieving parents, through years of high-pressure competition in school, and by that unyielding inner voice that keeps urging us to "Show 'em you can do it without anyone's help!"

The result, painful though it is to admit, is a lifestyle of impatience. We become easily irritated—often angry. We work longer hours. Take less time off. Forget how to laugh. And all the while the specter of discouragement looms across our horizon like a dark storm front—threatening to choke out any remaining sunshine.

My friend, it's time to declare it. You are not the Messiah of the twenty-first century! You are H-U-M-A-N . . . nothing more. So? Slow down. Give yourself a break. Stop trying to cover all three bases and sell popcorn in the stands at the same time. Relax for a change!

Once you've slowed down to neutral, crack open your Bible to Exodus 18 and read aloud verses 18–27 (NIV). It's the account of a visit Jethro made to the work place of his son-in-law . . . a fellow by the name of Moses. Old Jethro frowned as he watched Moses dash from one need to another, from one person to another. From early morning until late at night the harried leader of the Israelites was neck-deep in decisions and people-pressure. He must have looked very impressive—eating on the run, ripping from one end of the camp to the other, planning appointments, meeting deadlines.

But Jethro wasn't impressed. "What is this thing that you are doing for the people?" he asked. Moses was somewhat defensive as he attempted to justify his ridiculous schedule. Jethro didn't buy the story. Instead, he calmly advised his son-in-law against trying to do everything alone. He reproved him with strong words: "The thing that you are doing is not good. You will surely wear out. . . . "

In three words he told Moses to
CALL FOR HELP

The benefits of shifting and sharing the load? Read verses 22–23 for yourself. "It will be easier for you . . . you will be able to endure." That's interesting, isn't it? God wants our lifestyle to be easier than most of us realize.

When will we learn that efficiency is enhanced not by what we accomplish but more often by what we relinquish?

The world beginning to get you down? Feel rotten? Too tired to pray . . . in too big a hurry? Let me suggest one of the few four-letter words God loves to hear us shout when we're discouraged:

HELP!

ENCOURAGE ME

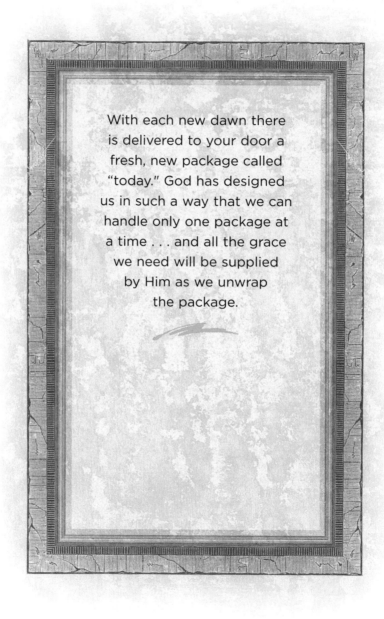

With each new dawn there
is delivered to your door a
fresh, new package called
"today." God has designed
us in such a way that we can
handle only one package at
a time . . . and all the grace
we need will be supplied
by Him as we unwrap
the package.

Make Space for Joy

R eal prayer—the kind of prayer Jesus mentioned and modeled— is realistic, spontaneous, down-to-earth communication with the living Lord that results in a relief of personal anxiety and a calm assurance that our God is in full control of our circumstances.

Our minds can be kept free of anxiety as we dump the load of our cares on the Lord in prayer. By getting rid of the stuff that drags us down, we create space for joy to take its place.

Think of it like this: Circumstances occur that could easily crush us. They may originate on the job or at home or even during the weekend when we are relaxing. Unexpectedly, they come. Immediately we have a choice to make . . . an attitude choice. We can hand the circumstances to God and ask Him to take control or we can roll up our mental sleeves and slug it out. Joy awaits our decision.

STRENGTHENING YOUR GRIP

AN ENCOURAGING WORD:

Thankfulness

It's amazing how you can
get delivered from worries
and woes and self-concern
when you start naming out
loud what you're thankful
for. Right away your focus
shifts from your needs
to the Father's mercy
and love.

Look at Life Through God's Eyes

Fears lurk in the shadows of every area of life. Perhaps you've suddenly discovered that an unexpected addition to your family is on the way. Don't be afraid. God can enable you to handle four kids just like He helped you handled three. You may be uncertain where your job is leading. The future may look very threatening. You are uneasy about what's around the corner. Or perhaps you have a doctor's appointment pending and you are afraid of what the exam might reveal. Jesus says, "Stop being afraid. Trust Me!"

One of the Greek terms for "tribulation" in the New Testament refers to "pressure . . . like being crushed under a big boulder." This is a description of pain, of enduring strain. It's an illustration of the crush of our times. There's a certain kind of pressure that comes with unemployment. There's another kind of pressure that comes with the threat of losing your home. There's a pressure that comes from sudden calamity or a rebellious child or a runaway mate. There's certainly pressure that comes with having too much to do and not having enough time to get it all done, a pressure that accompanies sleepless nights and the press of tomorrow's demanding responsibilities.

Jesus Christ stands at the door of your heart. He holds out His hands that are scarred. His feet are pierced, and He bears in His body the marks of death. He says, "I know the pressure you are under. I understand the strain. I know the unfair abuse. But let me offer you some encouragement. Don't be afraid. Look at life through My eyes! Stop letting life intimidate you! Stop running scared. Trust Me!"

PERFECT TRUST

The eyes of the LORD run to and fro throughout the whole earth, to show Himself strong on behalf of those whose heart is loyal to Him.

2 CHRONICLES 16:9 NKJV

What seems frustrating
and wrong and unfair is
not the end of the story.
It's just the end
of a chapter.

Chapter Five

ENCOURAGEMENT
FOR INJUSTICE AND
DISAPPOINTMENT

How to Keep Your Balance

D o you have an uncaring boss? Do you have a supervisor or a manager who isn't fair? Do you have to deal with unreasonable people? . . . The natural tendency of the human heart is to fight back against unfair and unreasonable treatment. But seeking revenge for unjust suffering can be a sign of self-appointed lordship over one's own affairs. Revenge, then, is totally inappropriate for one who has submitted to the lordship of Jesus Christ. Christians must stand in contrast to those around them. This includes a difference in attitude and a difference in focus. Our attitude should be "submissive," and our focus should be "toward God." And how is this change viewed by God? It "finds favor" with Him.

> If when you do what is right and suffer for it you patiently endure it, this finds favor with God.
>
> 1 PETER 2:20

There's no credit due a person who suffers for what he has coming to him. If you break into a house and steal, you will be arrested, and you could be incarcerated. And if you patiently endure your jail sentence, no one is going think you are wonderful for being such a good and patient prisoner. You won't get elected "Citizen of the Year."

But if you are a hard-working, faithful employee, diligent, honest, productive, prompt, caring, working for a boss who is belligerent, stubborn, short-sighted, and ungrateful, and if you patiently endure that situation—aha! That "finds favor" with God! Actually another meaning for the word translated "favor" is *grace*. So when you endure, you put grace on display. And when you put grace on display for the glory of God, you could revolutionize your workplace or any other situation.

Are you feeling the splinters of some cross of unjust suffering? Has a friend betrayed you? Has an employer impaled you? Has a disaster dropped on your life that's almost too great to bear? If so, don't fight back. Unjust suffering can be a dizzying experience. To keep your balance in those times when things are swirling around you, it's important to find a fixed reference point and focus on it. Return to the protection and guardianship of the Good Shepherd who endured the cross and laid down His life . . . for you.

HOPE AGAIN

Advantages in Disadvantages

S ad endings we can handle, but not unjust ones. Suffering makes us sad, but injustice makes us mad. In our child-like minds we still long for fairness and equity. We still want stories to end well so that people can live happily ever after. But life is not that neat and tidy. Only in fairy tales does right always triumph. In life, the helpless are pushed around, cruel people often get the slipper, and some of those we thought were generous, unselfish givers were actually, greedy, self-serving takers.

How do we deal with disadvantages, unfair treatment, and injustice? I think God's counsel, through Solomon, is remarkably on target:

> Nothing is better than that man should be
> happy in his activities, for that is his lot.
> For who will bring him to see what
> will occur after him?

ECCLESIASTES 3:22

Does he say, "Compare your lot with another person's and see how much better yours is than his?" Hardly. Does he say, "Retaliate, resent, become bitter; you didn't get a fair shake"? No way. Then *what* does he say? Namely this: Reject self-pity. Reject revenge. Reject resentment. Reject retaliation. Find ways to discover advantages to your disadvantages.

You and I constantly bump up against people submerged in self-pity. They are hopelessly lost in the swamp of discontent. All they can tell you is how wrong this was, how unfair she was, how someone's promise was broken, how that man walked away and left "me and the kids," that guy broke up a partnership and "took me to the cleaners," and on and on and on.

We usually can do very little to change our lot. We can only change our reaction to our lot. We cannot change our past, for example. I don't care how brilliant we are, our past stands in concrete. We cannot delete it. But we can learn today to see our past from God's perspective, and use the disadvantages of yesterday in our life—today and forever.

Some time ago I listened to the entire recording of a speech . . . something that I very seldom do. It was the tape of a speech delivered by a man named Tom Sullivan. He was addressing five thousand men and women in Dallas, as he spoke to the prestigious Million Dollar Round Table of the insurance companies around the world.

You may have seen Sullivan on the "Good Morning, America" program; he's one of their frequent guests. He's also done guest television appearances on "M-A-S-H" and "Fame." He was in the film *Airport '77*. He's a world-class athlete—with two national championship records in wrestling. He was on the 1958 Olympic wrestling team. He earned a degree at Harvard in clinical psychology. He's a musician. He's an author. He runs six miles a day on the beach. He swims. He sky dives . . . and has thirty-seven jumps to his credit. I should also tell you that Tom Sullivan is blind.

Five thousand successful insurance people were on the edge of their seats—applauding, enjoying, laughing, and learning—as they listened to a man who couldn't even see the podium in front of him, to say nothing of seeing the smiles on their faces.

He had one major point in his talk: "You've got a disadvantage? Take advantage of it! People don't buy similarity. They buy differences." The disadvantage is what makes you distinct and different. The similarities are no big deal.

What is your story? Everybody has a story. Sure, it's got some injustice in it. The message I want to leave with you is simply this: Disadvantages need not disqualify. Friend, let me ask you a question. When are you going to replace self-pity with courage? Imagine the lives you could reach and strengthen simply by being all you can be.

LIVING ON THE RAGGED EDGE

Beneficial

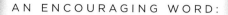

God knows the end from
the beginning, and He knows
you and your needs far better
than even you do. Don't ask,
"Why is this happening to me?"
Rather, ask the question,
"How should I respond?"
Otherwise, you'll miss
the beneficial role
suffering plays
in life.

God's Mercy

I n the Old Testament the Hebrew term for "mercy" is *chesed*.
It is a magnificent word, often translated "lovingkindness" or
simply "kindness."

> Surely goodness and lovingkindness
> will follow me all the days of my life,
> and I will dwell in the house
> of the LORD forever.

PSALM 23:6

God's goodness and lovingkindness—His *chesed*. His
mercy.

When I am treated unfairly, God's mercy relieves my
bitterness. That's what happens when *chesed* comes into my
cell. I have been in a dungeon of unfair treatment. Bitterness
becomes my enemy, but mercy relieves it. Mercy relieves my
heart of bitterness, and I can endure whatever comes my way.

When I grieve over loss, God's *chesed* relieves my anger.
Often that's the part of grief we don't want to admit—especially
anger against the one who has left us and anger against God

for taking our loved one. Mercy relieves our anger. Not instantly, but ultimately.

When I struggle with a disability, God's *chesed* relieves my self-pity. That can be a major enemy for the disabled— self-pity. When they finally come to terms with it in God's mercy, they are ready to do great things for God. But it takes mercy to get them over the hurdle of self-pity.

When I endure physical and/or emotional pain, *chesed* relieves my hopelessness. The great fear of those in long-lasting pain is hopelessness, the deep anguish that they cannot go on. That there'll never be a bright tomorrow. Relief seems gone forever.

When I deal with sinful actions, God's *chesed* relieves my guilt. Grace brings me forgiveness. Mercy relieves my guilt.

All the earthly struggles that occur are not accidents. God is in the midst of them, working out His sovereign will, granting us mercy. Mercy wrapped in love.

THE MYSTERY OF GOD'S WILL

Faithful

- When the X-ray comes back and it doesn't look good, remember, God is still faithful.

- When you read that heart-breaking note from your mate, remember, God is still faithful.

- When you hear the worst kind of news about one of your children, remember, God is still faithful. He has not abandoned you, though you're tempted to think He has.

In Good Hands

What does it mean to say that God is faithful? It means He is steadfast in His allegiance to His people. He will not leave us in the lurch. It also means He is firm in His adherence to His promises. He keeps His word. Faithfulness suggests the idea of loyalty: dependability; constancy; being resolute, steady, and consistent. God isn't fickle, no hot-and-cold temperamental moods with Him!

God is also faithful to remember His servants.

1. He remembers our work—each individual act.
2. He takes note of the love within us that prompted the deed.

No one on earth can do those special things. We forget, but God remembers. We see the action, God sees the motive. This qualifies Him as the best record keeper and judge. He alone is perfectly and consistently just. You're in good hands with the Almighty!

IMPROVING YOUR SERVE

The pursuit of happiness is the cultivation of a Christ-centered, Christ-controlled life.

A Bunch of Nobodies

Pull a sheet of scratch paper out of your memory bank and see how well you do with the following questions:

Who taught Martin Luther his theology and inspired his translation of the New Testament?

Who visited Dwight L. Moody at a shoe store and spoke to him about Christ?

Who was the elderly women who prayed faithfully for Billy Graham for over twenty years?

Who financed William Carey's ministry in India?

Who refreshed the apostle Paul in that Roman dungeon as he wrote his last letter to Timothy?

Who followed Hudson Taylor and gave the China Inland Mission its remarkable vision and direction?

Who were the parents of the godly and gifted prophet Daniel?

Okay, how did you do? Over fifty percent? Maybe twenty-five percent? Not quite that good?

Before you excuse your inability to answer the questions by calling the quiz "trivia," better stop and think. Had it not been for those unknown people—those "nobodies"—a huge chunk of church history would be missing. And a lot of lives would have been untouched.

Nobodies.

What a necessary band of men and women . . . servants of the King . . . yet nameless in the kingdom! Men and women who, with silent heroism, yet faithful diligence, relinquish the limelight and live in the shade of public figures.

What was it Jim Elliot, the martyred messenger of the gospel to the Aucas, once called missionaries? Something like *a bunch of nobodies trying to exalt Somebody.*

But don't mistake anonymous for *unnecessary.* Otherwise the whole Body of believers gets crippled . . . even paralyzed . . . or, at best, terribly dizzy as the majority of the members become diseased with self-pity and discouragement. Face it, friend, the Head of the Body calls the shots. It is His prerogative to publicize some and hide others. Don't ask me why He chooses whom He uses.

If it's His desire to use you as a Melanchthon rather than a Luther . . . or a Kimball rather than a Moody . . . or an Onesiphorus rather than a Paul . . . or a Hoste rather than a Taylor, relax!

Better than that, give God praise! You're among that elite group mentioned in 1 Corinthians 12 as:

> . . . some of the parts that seem weakest and least
> important are really the most necessary. . . . So God
> has put the body together in such a way that extra
> honor and care are given to those parts that
> might otherwise seem less important.

VV. 22, 24 TLB

Nobodies . . . exalting Somebody.

Are you one? Listen to me! It's the "nobodies" Somebody chooses so carefully. And when He has selected you for that role, *He* does not consider you a nobody.

Be encouraged!

ENCOURAGE ME

Laughter

Jesus took the twelve disciples
across a lake to enjoy some
rest and relaxation alone on
a mountainside. Who knows
what they did for fun? Maybe
they swam or sat around a
campfire and told a few jokes.
Whatever, you can count
on this—they laughed.

We all look so much better
and feel so much better
when we laugh. I don't know
of a more contagious sound.

Take Heart!

I t is so easy to feel used and unappreciated.

Do I write to you who serve behind the scenes in a ministry or a business? You work faithfully and diligently, yet the glory goes to another. Your efforts make someone else successful. How easy to feel resentful! Assistant directors, associate and assistant pastors, administrative assistants, "internal personnel." All members of the I-work-hard-but-because-I'm-not-up-front-I-never-get-the-credit club, take heart! Our God who rewards in secret will never overlook your commitment.

Keep a close eye on your pride. God's true servant is like the Lord Jesus, who came not "to be served, but to serve, and to give His life a ransom for many" (Mark 10:45). . . . When you make the stew and someone else gets the strokes, remember your role: to serve and to give.

> God is not unjust so as to forget your work and
> the love which you have shown toward His name.
>
> HEBREWS 6:10

IMPROVING YOUR SERVE

Reach for God's Hand

D o you ever find yourself saying something like this? "Lord, I give You my life, but I'm weary to death of this irritation, this person, this circumstance, this uncomfortable situation. I feel trapped, Lord. I want relief—I *must* have relief! And if You don't bring it soon . . . well, I've had it. I feel like walking away from it all."

You may walk, my friend, but there are no shortcuts. Here's a better plan: Reach for the hand of your Guide! He is Lord of the desert. Even your desert. The most precious object of God's love is His child in the desert. If it were possible, you mean more to Him during this time than at any other time. You are as the pupil of His eye. You are His beloved student taking His toughest courses. He loves you with an infinite amount of love.

Jesus went through the worst desert of all for you. He was alone as no man has ever been alone. He was rejected. He lived in obscurity. He suffered the worst earth and hell could hurl at Him. On the cross He said, "I thirst." And when that desert night was the darkest, He screamed, "My God My God, Why have you forsaken Me?"

Jesus walked through the desert first. He felt its heat. He tasted its loneliness. He accepted its obscurity. He faced down Satan himself while the desert winds howled around Him. And He will never, ever forget or forsake the one who follows Him across the sand.

MOSES: A MAN OF SELFLESS DEDICATION

Since God has "an appointed time for everything," an ideal method of time management is **T-R-U-S-T**, putting the pressure back into His hands.

Beautiful in Its Time

Among Christians a favorite verse of Scripture is Romans 8:28.

> *"And we know that God causes all things to work together for good to those who love God, to those who are called according to His purpose."*

The key part of the verse is "work together." That verse does not say "all things are good." It says, "All things are good as they work together for His purpose." A similar thought was written by Solomon in Ecclesiastes 3:11: *"He makes everything appropriate in its time."* The Hebrew word translated *appropriate* means "beautiful." Notice Solomon's comment does not say "everything is beautiful." It says "beautiful *in its time*." God has made everything beautiful in its time.

And I've got news for those who struggle with God's timing. You may not live to see God's time completely fulfilled. You may live to a ripe old age, carry out your reason for existence, and die before the full program of God has reached

its ultimate and completed purpose. But His promise stands—
He will make everything beautiful in its time.

Quite frankly, our problem is that we focus our attention
on the wrong thing. We see the fuzzy, ugly cocoon; God plans
and sets in motion the butterfly. We see the painful, awful
process; He is producing the value of the product. We see
today; He is working on forever. We get caught up in the
wrapping; He focuses on the gift, the substance down inside.
We look at the external; He emphasizes the internal. He makes
everything beautiful in its time, including your loss, your
hospital experience, your failures, your brokenness, your
battles, your fragmented dreams, your lost romance, your
heartache, your illness. Yes, even your terminal illness. And
one more word on this, God wouldn't say "everything" if He
didn't mean "everything." That includes whatever you're going
through. He makes it beautiful in its time. Without Him, life is
purposeless and profitless, miserable and meaningless. With
Him, it will ultimately make sense.

LIVING ON THE RAGGED EDGE

Act in Faith

Trusting God doesn't alter our circumstances. Perfect trust in Him changes *us*. It doesn't make life all rosy and beautiful and neat and lovely and financially secure and comfortable. But trust that is rooted in an abiding faith in God makes all that real in us—secure, relaxed, and calm against insuperable odds.

You know one of the most encouraging things about faith? *It pleases God*. In fact,

Without faith it is impossible to please Him.

HEBREW 11:6

That's why I want to encourage you: Walk by faith! Stop this plagued biting of nails and weariness of worry that you encourage within when the tests come. Relax! Learn to say, "Lord, this is Your battle. This is Your need that You've allowed me to trust You for. And I'm waiting for You to do it. I'm willing to wait as long as necessary for You to do the impossible."

When God sees this kind of faith He smiles in return and responds, "I'm, ready to support you. Give Me that need! Cast it on Me!" He stands ready to "support those whose heart is completely His" (2 Chronicles 16:9). These are the kind of people God is searching for: People who act in faith. People whose lives are being turned right side up through perfect trust.

PERFECT TRUST

In quietness and
confidence shall be
your strength.

ISAIAH 30:15 NKJV

"God Is There and He Is Not Silent"

R egardless of rank, status, color, creed, age, heritage,
intelligence, or temperament, the "hand of God" is
upon us. The late philosopher-theologian Francis Schaeffer
was absolutely correct: "God is there and He is not silent."
What reassurance this brings! It tells us, among other things,
that nothing is out of control. Nor are we useless, despairing
robots stumbling awkwardly through time and space, facing a
bleak fate at the end. But neither does this mean we are given
periodic briefings about His strategy. . . .

Being in the hand of God is not synonymous with or a
guarantee for being economically prosperous, physically healthy,
protected from pain, enjoying a trouble-free occupation, and
having everyone smile and appreciate us. As Solomon wrote
"man does not know whether it will be love or hatred; anything
awaits him." But what does help is the knowledge that behind
whatever happens is a God who cares, who hasn't lost a handle
on the controls.

LIVING ON THE RAGGED EDGE

Every day God
says to our world,
"All is forgiven . . .
come on home."

Chapter Six

ENCOURAGEMENT
FOR MISTAKES
AND FAILURES

Full Forgiveness

It happens to every one of us. Teachers as well as students. Bosses as well as assistants. Parents as well as kids. The diligent as well as the lazy. Not even presidents are immune. Or corporation heads who earn six-figure salaries.

What happens? Making mistakes, that's what. Doing the wrong thing, usually with the best of motives. And it happens with remarkable regularity.

Let's face it, success is overrated. All of us crave it despite daily proof that man's real genius lies in quite the opposite direction. It's really incompetence that we're all pros at. Which brings me to a basic question that has been burning inside me for months: How come we're so surprised when we see it in others and so devastated when it has occurred in ourselves?

Show me the guy who wrote the rules for perfectionism and I'll guarantee he's a nail-biter with a face full of tics . . . whose wife dreads to see him come home. Furthermore, he forfeits the right to be respected because he's either guilty of not admitting he blew it or he has become an expert at cover-up.

You can do that, you know. Stop and think of ways certain

people can keep from coming out and confessing they blew it. Doctors can bury their mistakes. Lawyer's mistakes get shut up in prison—literally. Dentists' mistakes are pulled. Carpenters turn theirs into sawdust.

Hey, there have been some real winners! Back in 1957, Ford bragged about "the car of the decade." The Edsel. Unless you lucked out, the Edsel you bought had a door that wouldn't close, a hood that wouldn't open, a horn that kept getting stuck, paint that peeled, and a transmission that failed to fulfill its mission. One business writer likened the Edsel's sales graph to an extremely dangerous ski slop. He added that so far as he knew, there was only one case on record of an Edsel ever being stolen!

A friend of mine, realizing how adept I am in this business of blowing it, passed on to me an amazing book (accurate, but funny) entitled *The Incomplete Book of Failures* by Stephen Pile. Appropriately, the book itself had two missing pages when it was printed, so the first thing you read is an apology for the omission—and an erratum slip that provides the two pages.

The only thing we can be thankful for when it comes to blowing it is that nobody keeps a record of ours. Or do they? Or do you with *others?* Not if you are serious about encouragement.

Come on, ease off. If our perfect Lord is gracious enough to take our worst, our ugliest, our most boring, our least successful, our Edsel flops, and forgive them, burying them in the depths of the sea, then it's high time we give each other a break.

In fact, He promises full acceptance along with full forgiveness in print for all to read . . . without an erratum sheet attached. Isn't that encouraging? Can't we be that type of encourager to one another? After all, imperfection is one of the few things we still have in common.

ENCOURAGE ME

AN ENCOURAGING WORD:

Grace

Don't waste your time
focusing on what you used
to be. Remember, the hope we
have in Christ means there's
a brighter tomorrow. Confession
and repentance renew our
relationsiop with our God.
The sins are forgiven. The
shame is canceled out.
We're no longer chained
to a deep, dark pit of
the past. Grace gives
us wings to soar.

Learning and Growing

We hardly need the reminder that the Christian life is not a cloud-nine utopia. And if you think it is, then I am going to burst that balloon once and for all. Because that's not only a terribly unrealistic view, thinking that Christ helps you "live happily ever after"; it's downright unbiblical! Once we're in heaven, sure, that's a different story. But until then, there are not many days you could write in your journal: fantastic, unbelievable, incredible, remarkable. Most of life is learning and growing, falling and getting back up, forgiving and forgetting, accepting and going on. . . .

God is the Potter, we are the clay. He is the one who gives the commands; we are the ones who obey. He never has to explain Himself; He never has to ask permission. He is shaping us into the image of His Son, regardless of the pain and heartache that may require. Those lessons are learned a little easier when we remember that we are not in charge.

THE MYSTERY OF GOD'S WILL

"My thoughts are not your thoughts,
Nor are your ways My ways,"
declares the LORD.

"For as the heavens are higher
than the earth,
So are My ways higher
than your ways
And My thoughts than
your thoughts."

ISAIAH 55:8–9

The Warmth of God's Love

Frequently through the Scriptures, references to light and sunshine are used to describe the warmth of God's love. "The LORD is my light and my salvation. Whom shall I fear?" (Psalm 27:1) asked the psalmist. When we are enveloped in the warmth of our Father's love, we fear no one. It gives us a sense of invincible security to be under His wings, surrounded by His care.

The light of God's ever-present, always-comforting love is pleasant. And it's good for our eyes to focus on the warmth and protection of the hand of God wrapped around our lives and to know that He is pleased with us and that He gives us permission to enjoy ourselves. When we focus on Him, He lifts the gloom and begins to lift the pounding pain of depression.

LIVING ON THE RAGGED EDGE

No one wants to be shipwrecked.
But the reality is, it happens,
not only on the open
sea, but also in life.

The secret of victory at sea
is what you do ahead of time
in calmer waters. If your life is
storm-free as you read this book,
I urge you to take advantage of
the peaceful lull. Spend time in
God's Word. Deepen your walk
with Him through prayer and
personal worship. Then, when
the inevitable winds of
adversity begin to blow
you'll be ready to
respond in faith,
rather than fear.

AN ENCOURAGING WORD:

Forgiveness

When we repent, God
promises restitution and
forgiveness through the
blood of Jesus Christ.

If we confess our sins,
He is faithful and righteous
to forgive us our sins
and to cleanse us from
all unrighteousness.

1 JOHN 1:9

Stop and Listen

My car has warning lights on the dashboard. Every once in a while when I am driving, one of them flashes bright red. When it does, I do not respond by pulling over and getting a little hammer out of the glove box and knocking out the light so that I can drive without being distracted. No, I stop and turn the engine off. In fact, I've had mechanics say, "Never just keep driving when your warning lights light up. Stop and find somebody to give you some help."

God has His own warning lights, and at times He flashes them, saying to us, "Stop, stop, don't, don't!" And if we're wise, we stop. We don't just let go and say, "Well, He's going to have to take care of it." We take care of it. "We confess our sins and He is faithful and just to forgive us our sins." We use the necessary disciplines that keep our minds pure, and He does His part in honoring that obedience.

We don't passively yawn our way through life hoping by the grace of God that we'll somehow make it. In His strength, we supply self-control, we supply perseverance, and in our perseverance, godliness. (2 Peter 1:5–8)

THE MYSTERY OF GOD'S WILL

You are God, ready
to pardon, gracious
and merciful.

NEHEMIAH 9:17 NKJV

AN ENCOURAGING WORD:

Love

The most precious object
of God's love is His child in the
desert. If it were possible, you
mean more to Him during this
time than at any other time.
You are His beloved student
taking his toughest courses.
He loves you with an infinite
amount of love. In our deepest
times, His love is our oasis . . .
and it's never a mirage.

Living by Faith

If you think you've got to be a certain type of person to live by faith, you're sadly mistaken. Consider the list of examples of faith God highlights for us in Hebrews chapter eleven . . .

Consider Noah. He was a farmer, but he went into the boat-building business for a period of 120 years. Then there is Abraham. He was a businessman raised by idolatrous parents. He was not a prophet. He was "just a businessman." And how about Sarah? She was a homemaker, plain and simple. She wasn't a prophetess or a woman preacher. She was a homemaker, but she was included in the inspired record as a woman of faith. There's also Joseph. He was a slave with a prison record, but then he became a prime minister. Moses was a shepherd who worked for his father-in-law, out in the desert. He didn't do a thing that was spiritually significant for eighty years! And what about Rahab, the harlot? How can a woman from that kind of background be a woman of faith? Well, ask God. He is responsible for the record.

PERFECT TRUST

God is not going to replace
suffering with glory;
rather He will transform
suffering into glory.

Chapter Seven

ENCOURAGEMENT
FOR SUFFERING
AND SORROW

The Perfect Result

Trials come in various categories.

They may be physical, emotional, financial, relational, or spiritual. They may slip in unexpectedly and knock on the door of your business, your church, or your home. They may arrive at any time or at any season. They may come suddenly, like a car accident or a natural catastrophe. They may be prolonged, like a drawn-out court case or a lingering, nagging illness. Trials can be public in nature or very private. They can be directly related to our own sin, the sin of others, or not related to sin at all.

A trial can be like a rock hitting the water. You don't cause the jolt, but you're impacted by it. You're just standing there, and suddenly the smooth lake of your life surges into giant waves and almost drowns you.

Frankly, some trials seem to blow in absolutely without reason. My brother, Orville, encountered something like that when a hurricane named Andrew blew through the community where he lived in south Florida a few years ago. It tore and ripped and screamed its way through, tearing his house apart. He had a great attitude, though. He called and said, "What an experience! It really did a lot of damage. But the good news is it tore down everyone's fences, so now we'll get to meet our neighbors."

"Consider it all joy, my brethren, when you encounter various trials, knowing that the testing of your faith produces endurance. And let endurance have its perfect result, so that you may be perfect and complete, lacking in nothing".

JAMES 1:2–4

James says we experience trials so that we may be become "perfect and complete," like a plant that has matured to its maximum growth and fruitfulness. That, he says, is the "perfect result" of "endurance."

Most often, because of the discomfort, the pain, or the hardship, we try to cut our trials short—to put an end to them. Before long, we're resenting them to such an extreme that we'll try anything to escape, to run from them. Instead, James says, endure the trial; let it come to completion. When it does, you'll be a better person for it.

HOPE AGAIN

Nothing touches me that has not passed through the hands of my heavenly Father. Nothing. Whatever occurs, God has sovereignly surveyed and approved. We may not know why (we may never know why), but we do know our pain is no accident to Him who guides our lives.

Accept and Trust

We don't look alike. We don't act alike. We don't dress alike. We have different tastes in the food we eat, the books we read, the cars we drive, and the music we enjoy. You like opera; I like country. We have dissimilar backgrounds, goals, and motivations. We work at different jobs, and we enjoy different hobbies. You like rock climbing; I like Harleys. We ascribe to a variety of philosophies and differ over politics. We have our own unique convictions on child-rearing and education. Our weights vary. Our heights vary. So does the color of our skin.

But there is one thing we all have in common: We all know what it means to hurt.

Suffering is a universal language. Tears are the same for Jews or Muslims or Christians, for white or black or brown, for children or adults or the elderly. When life hurts and our dreams fade, we may express our anguish in different ways, but each one of us knows the sting of pain and heartache, disease and disaster, trials and sufferings.

Joseph Parker, a great preacher of yesteryear, once said to a group of aspiring young ministers, "Preach to the suffering and you will never lack a congregation. There is a broken heart in every pew."

Truly, suffering is the common thread in all our garments.

Can you imagine going through such times without Jesus Christ? I can't. But frankly, that's what most people do. They face those frightening fears and sleepless nights in the hospital without Christ. They struggle with a wayward teenager without Christ. Alone, they endure the awful words from a mate, "I don't want to live with you any longer. I want my freedom. I don't love you any more. I'm gone." And they go through it all without Christ.

For souls like these, life is one painful sting after another. But those who are "born again" in the Lord Jesus Christ have been promised a living hope through His resurrection from the dead.

So if you want to smile through your tears, if you want to rejoice through times of suffering, just keep reminding yourself that, as a Christian, what you're going through isn't the end of the story . . . it's simply the rough journey that leads to the right destination.

Two words will help you cope when you run low on hope: *accept* and *trust*. Accept the mystery of hardship, suffering, misfortune, or mistreatment. Don't try to understand it or explain it. Accept it. Then, deliberately trust God to protect you by His power from this very moment to the dawning of eternity.

Paul had a thorn in the flesh, and he prayed three times for God to remove it. "No," said God, "I'm not taking it away." Finally Paul said, "I've learned to trust in You, Lord. I've learned to live with it." It was then God said, "My grace is sufficient for that thorn." He matched the color of the test with the color of grace.

When we are suffering, only Christ's perspective can replace our resentment with rejoicing. I've seen it happen in hospital rooms. I've seen it happen in families. I've seen it happen in my own life.

Our whole perspective changes when we catch a glimpse of the purpose of Christ in it all. Take that away, and it's nothing more than a bitter, terrible experience.

Suffering comes in many forms and degrees, but His grace is always there to carry us beyond it. I've lived long enough and endured a sufficient number of trials to say without hesitation that only Christ's perspective can replace our resentment with rejoicing. Jesus is the central piece of suffering's puzzle. If we fit Him into place, the rest of the puzzle—no matter how complex and enigmatic—begins to make sense.

HOPE AGAIN

My grace is sufficient
for you, for power is
perfected in weakness.

2 CORINTHIANS 12:9

AN ENCOURAGING WORD:

Trust

At times God's plan will frighten
you. Or you'll be intimidated by
its demands. Other times you'll
be disappointed. For instance,
when God tells you no, to wait, or
to sit tight, you'll want to argue.
You may decide to fight. You
might attempt to negotiate.
You may pout and become
angry. But when your faith
kicks in gear, none of those
impulses will control you. Faith
says, "I can do this. I trust you,
Lord. I don't understand everything, but I trust you completely."

How God Works Through Suffering

God . . . comforts us in all our
affliction so that we may be able to
comfort those who are in any affliction with
the comfort with which we ourselves
are comforted by God.

2 CORINTHIANS 1:3–4

In 2 Corinthians chapter one, three reasons are given for suffering. Admittedly, there may be dozens of other reasons, but here are three specific reasons God allows suffering:

➤ that we might have the capacity to enter into others' sorrow and affliction;

➤ that we might learn what it means to depend on Him;

➤ that we might learn to give thanks in everything.

Specific pain enables us to comfort others specifically. If you lose your child, God uses you in the life of a mother as she endures the loss of her child. If you've struggled through the dark tunnel of divorce, no one understands as you do when a friend tells you a spouse has just walked out the door.

I've never had cancer. I couldn't offer the depth of comfort you could if you've had that disease. That's how God works.

FIVE MEANINGFUL MINUTES A DAY

"Shall we indeed accept
good from God and not
accept adversity?"

JOB 2:10

AN ENCOURAGING WORD:

Hope

One of the great themes of
Christianity is triumphant hope.
Not just hope as in a distant,
vague dream, but triumphant
hope, the kind of hope where
all things end right. In the midst
of the struggles and the storms
and the sufferings of life, we
can advance our thoughts
beyond today and see relief
. . . triumph . . . victory.
Because, in the end,
God does indeed win.

The Savior Is by Your Side

You and I enter this world screaming. Physicians tell us that one of the first signs of good, healthy lungs in newborns is that initial, piercing cry. The tiny child whose little frame squeezes his way through a narrow birth canal, screeches in pain when he leaves the warmth of the womb and emerges with a gush into the cold, cruel world—a world of pain.

From the moment we're born until our final breath, pain is our companion, albeit one we'd choose to abandon.

But may I remind you that you cannot have a heartache Jesus doesn't understand and with which He doesn't identify. You cannot have a physical pain that somehow escapes His awareness. You cannot have a crippling disease, a disability, a grief, a heart murmur or full-on heart attack . . . not even a debilitating fear or panic attack that He cannot understand or feel. He's felt it all. Therefore He's there to walk with you through your most profound depths of pain, if you'll only let Him.

Do you have a lingering scar within you that won't heal? Look at His hands, His feet, and His side. Feeling humiliated and alone? He knows what that feels like. Are you so confused by your circumstances that you're tempted to bargain with God for relief? No need. Without one word from your lips, He understands. He's touched with the feelings of our weaknesses, and therefore He identifies with them.

Perhaps you're lonely. Your lifelong mate has gone to be with the Lord. You face an uncertain future—all alone. You may have recently been forgotten. Maybe your parents told you to get out of their lives. Perhaps your husband or your wife just walked out for good, rejecting you for someone else. Or you may have just read a cruel letter from an adult child that included seven words you cannot bear to believe: "I never want to see you again." Relationally, you need somebody. Internally, you're in anguish. Physically, you've reached your threshold.

You may be confused, living with deep emotional scars as a result of being abused. You may suffer from such a horrible and shameful addiction that you fear rejection by anyone who might discover your secret. The pain of shame grips your soul and ambushes your thoughts. Today, you may feel helpless, enraged, confused, disappointed, depressed, misunderstood, humiliated, and at the end.

Ultimately you wonder why God has forsaken you. You may feel that, but hear this: you are not alone. There is hope. There is help with the Savior by your side.

Physically, no one comforts better than Christ. In the midst of your deepest physical pain, His presence brings comfort and strength. He may choose to restore your physical health, but frankly, He may not. Regardless, His grace is abundantly sufficient for you. His hand is on your life at this time of your affliction. It's better than the hand of any friend, any partner, any parent, or any child, because when He touches, He brings great compassion and lasting relief. No one comforts better than Christ.

Ultimately, no one sees the benefits of our pain clearer than Christ. He sees through the dark, winding tunnel of your Gethsemane all the way to the end. You see only the unrelenting, frightening, thick darkness. He sees beyond it into the shining light of eternity. Maturity, growth, stability, wisdom, and ultimately the crown of life await the one who trusts His unseen hand. Keep in mind, He owns the map that guides you through your Gethsemane.

"Man of Sorrows," what a name! It's the name of the Son of God. His name is Jesus.

GETTING THROUGH THE TOUGH STUFF

Putting Things Into Perspective

M any years ago a longtime friend of mine, Dr. Robert Lightner, was involved in a terrible plane crash. He was in a single-engine plane that flipped over during takeoff. He was badly injured and bruised beyond recognition. His wife, Pearl, said that when she first saw him at the hospital, "I looked at this black mass of flesh, and I didn't even know who he was." Thankfully, he did recover, and today he is a living testimony of the grace of God through that ordeal. "I learned things I didn't know I needed to learn," I heard him say on one occasion. Isn't that the way it usually is?

Some of you are going through trials right now that have dropped you on your knees. At the same time those trials are pulling you closer to the Lord than you've ever been in your life. That ought to bring rejoicing. You'll be more closely linked to Him. Some of the mysterious themes threaded through His Word will become clearer because you have been leveled by some unexpected affliction or enduring persecution or facing misunderstanding.

HOPE AGAIN

AN ENCOURAGING WORD:

Comfort

Sometimes you just don't feel
like singing or smiling. Matter
of fact, there are times it's
hypocritical to paste a smile
on your face. So don't.

It is in those times that I
am most thankful for the
Scriptures. In God's Word we
not only discover His will for our
lives, we find words of genuine
comfort for those times when
life comes unglued.

Every journey is
accomplished one
step at at time.

AN ENCOURAGING WORD:

Companionship

When the barometer of life
drops to the bottom of the
gauge—when the winds of
adversity blow hard against
our souls, we cannot make it on
our own. We not only need the
Lord, we need each other.

- When we are lonely, we need an understanding friend. Jesus is the one who "sticks closer than a brother."

- When we are lonely, we need strength to keep putting one foot in front of the other—Jesus is the One "who strengthens me."

- When we are lonely, we need to lift our eyes off ourselves. Jesus, the "Author and Finisher" of the life of faith, invites us to fix our eyes on Him.

The Mystery of God's Mercy

I have a physician friend who stayed by his wife's side for almost a year as she was dying with ovarian cancer. He told me of such occasions, when the Lord gave merciful relief from the pain. He said, "It was almost as if an angel of mercy hovered over our room."

When we're suffering the consequences of unfair treatment, there is mercy with God. When we're enduring the grief of loss, there is mercy. When we struggle with the limitations of a disability, there is mercy. When we're hurting and in physical pain, there is mercy. All these earthly struggles that occur are no accident. God is in the midst of them, working out His sovereign will. Yes, it's a mystery, which means we need special mercy to endure the anguish and misery of the pain.

> Bless the LORD, O my soul, . . . Who crowns
> you with loving-kindness and compassion.
>
> PSALM 103:1, 4

The sovereign Most High God is ruler over our lives. So it's obvious that if we ever have the feeling of relief, God has given it to us. He's the author of relief. He's the one who grants us the peace, the satisfaction, the ease. In fact, I think relief is a wonderful synonym for mercy. Mercy is God's active compassion, which He demonstrates on behalf of the miserable. When we are in a time of deep distress and God activates His compassion to bring about relief, we've experienced mercy.

THE MYSTERY OF GOD'S WILL

You are secure
in God's hands.

CLOSING
THOUGHTS

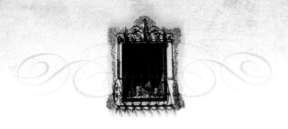

Searching for Shelter

D *iscouragement.*
    Where does it come from?

Sometimes it feels like a dry, barren wind off a lonely desert. And something inside us begins to wilt.

At other times it feels like a chilling mist. Seeping through our pores, it numbs the spirit and fogs the path before us.

What is it about discouragement that strips our lives of joy and leaves us feeling vulnerable and exposed?

I don't know all the reasons. I don't even know most of the reasons. But I do know *one* of the reasons: We don't have a refuge. Shelters are hard to come by these days . . . you know, people who care enough to listen. Who are good at keeping secrets. And we all need harbors to pull into when we feel weather-worn and blasted by the storm.

What do you need when circumstances punch a hole in your dike and threaten to engulf your life with pain and confusion?

You need a shelter. A listener. Someone who understands.

But to whom do you turn when there's no one to tell your troubles to? Where do you find encouragement?

I'd like to call to your attention a man who turned to the living Lord and found in Him a place to rest and repair. His name was David. Cornered, bruised by adversity, and struggling with feeling rejected, he wrote these words in his journal of woes:

> In you, O LORD, I have taken refuge;
> Let me never be ashamed; in your
> righteousness deliver me.
> Incline Your ear to me,
> rescue me quickly;
> be to me a rock of strength,
> a stronghold to save me.
>
> PSALM 31:1–2

David declares his need for a "refuge." The Hebrew term speaks of a protective place, a place of safety, security, secrecy. In God, David found encouragement.

Why not share David's shelter? The One he called My Strength, Mighty Rock, Fortress, Stronghold, and High Tower.

David's Refuge *never* failed. Not even once.

ENCOURAGE ME

He is Lord of the
unexpected and the
unpredictable. Our times
and our trials are
in His hands.

He Promises Himself

D o you have a problem? You're smiling back at me. "A problem? Would you believe *several dozen* problems?" If you listen to the voices around you, you'll search for a substitute—an escape route. You'll miss the fact that each of those problems is a God-appointed instructor ready to stretch you and challenge you and deepen your walk with Him.

It's inevitable. We continually encounter hardships. People disappoint us. We disappoint ourselves. But God is constant and compassionate. We are not alone. He cares. Against all reason, the transcendent God loves us so much that He has committed Himself to us.

The question is: are we committed to Him? If you wish to be a man or woman of God who desires to live a godly life that will leave its mark upon this world, you must stand in the shadow of your Savior. Trust Him to work through the trials you encounter, through the extreme circumstances you cannot handle on your own. He is still the God of impossible situations. He does what no earthly individual can do.

Remember, He is fully aware of the trials in your life. The next time your life is filled with God-appointed storms, two things should comfort you. First, these squalls surge across *everyone's* horizon. Second, we all *need* them. God has no other method more effective. The massive blows and shattering blasts (not to mention the little, constant irritations) smooth us, humble us, and compel us to submit to *His* script and *His* chosen role for our lives.

Wherever you are in this journey called life, wherever you may be employed, wherever you may be in your domestic situation, wherever you may be in your age, your health, or your lifestyle, God may be preparing you for a great surprise in order to find you faithful. Rather than running from Him, let me suggest the opposite: Run *toward* Him.

Are you weary? Guilty? Distressed? Come to the Savior. Come immediately, come repeatedly, come boldly. And be at rest. When was the last time you came to the Lord, all alone, and gave Him your load of care? God does not dispense strength and encouragement like a druggist fills a prescription. The Lord doesn't promise to give us something to *take* so we can handle our weary moments. He promises us *Himself*. That is all. And that is enough.

Charles R. Swindoll

Acknowledgments

G rateful acknowledgment is made to the following publishers for permission to reprint this copyrighted material. All copyrights are held by the author, Charles R. Swindoll.

Improving Your Serve (Nashville: Word, 1981).
Encourage Me: Caring Words for Heavy Hearts (Grand Rapids: Zondervan Publishing House, 1982).
Strengthening Your Grip (Nashville: W Publishing Group, 1982).
Dropping Your Guard (Nashville: W. Publishing Group, 1983).
Living on the Ragged Edge (Nashville: W Publishing Group, 1985).
Laugh Again (Nashville: W Publishing Group, 1994).
Hope Again (Nashville: W Publishing Group, 1996).
The Mystery of God's Will (Nashville: W Publishing Group, 1999).
Moses: A Man of Selfless Dedication (Nashville: W Publishing Group, 1999).
Perfect Trust (Nashville: J. Countryman, 2000).
Elijah: A Man of Heroism and Humility (Nashville: W Publishing, 2000).
Five Meaningful Minutes a Day (Nashville: J Countryman, 2003)
Getting Through the Tough Stuff (Nashville: W Publishing, 2004)